Charles Rogers

Scottish Branch of the Norman House of Roger

With a genealogical sketch of the family of Playfair

Charles Rogers

Scottish Branch of the Norman House of Roger
With a genealogical sketch of the family of Playfair

ISBN/EAN: 9783337243791

Printed in Europe, USA, Canada, Australia, Japan

Cover: Foto ©ninafisch / pixelio.de

More available books at **www.hansebooks.com**

THE SCOTTISH BRANCH

OF THE

NORMAN HOUSE OF ROGER

With a Genealogical Sketch

OF THE

FAMILY OF PLAYFAIR

BY THE

Rev. CHARLES ROGERS, LL.D., F.S.A. Scot.

Historiographer to the Historical Society.

LONDON:

PRINTED FOR PRIVATE CIRCULATION.

1872.

THE research of a quarter of a century connected with the history of one family, and of a portion of another, is represented in these pages. That research has been more genealogical than biographical,—necessarily so, for to the majority of those commemorated apply the poet's lines,—

> " Along the cool sequester'd vale of life,
> They kept the noiseless tenor of their way."

Even of the more conspicuous members, memoirs have not been attempted ; these may be found in the ordinary channels. To family traditions no heed has been paid. The narrative is a severe relation of authenticated facts.

All well-informed persons acknowledge the influence of race. The civilization of Western Europe was effected by the Celts, Saxons, and Normans—successively the pioneers, planters, and polishers of cultivated life. The great Houses of the United Kingdom claim Norman descent. Those families which constitute the better portion of the middle class trace to a Scandinavian ancestry. The Saxon and Norman races as surely reach the upper strata of society, as does cream top the milk-pail or oil rise upon water.

The Family of Roger, which forms the main subject of these pages, is one of the very few Scottish Houses which have acquired a surname from a conversion of the personal name of its founder into that use. Belonging to a ruling race, the members have always cherished a stubborn independence, and though rarely affluent, have never suffered social degradation. Some of the members are known to have been firm and resolute of purpose, but none have been other than humane, beneficent, and generous.

With the Scottish House of Roger the family of Playfair has, by frequent intermarriage, become closely identified. The precise origin of the House of Playfair has not been ascertained. The Rev. Andrew Playfair, Minister of Aberdalgie, Perthshire, from 1613 to 1658, is the first Scotsman of the race of whom I know anything. He left a son Andrew, who may have settled in Perthshire; yet I incline to believe that he was not the founder of the Bendochy family; a brother of the clergyman is more likely, for the Christian name Andrew does not even once occur among the numerous members of the sept recorded in the Bendochy Registers. The Minister of Aberdalgie accepted ordination from the Bishop of Dunkeld (Dr. Scott's *Fasti*). This fact argues Anglican proclivities. John Playfere, Doctor of Divinity, Fellow of St. John's College, Cambridge, and Margaret Professor of Divinity about the year 1596, composed a work on Predestination, which was published posthumously, and has been reprinted. The name Playfere, or Playfair, is clearly a corruption of Playford, a compound word plainly indicating that its first owners hied from the plains of Scandinavia.

SNOWDOUN VILLA,
LEWISHAM, S.E.,
February, 1872.

THE SCOTTISH HOUSE OF ROGER, Etc.

SEVERAL centuries before the introduction of surnames, and its adoption as a family designation, the name of Roger was common over Europe. It is still to be found, both as a christian and a family name, in most of the continental countries. In France it is spelt Roger; in German Roger and Rüdiger; in Norway Hrodgjer and Ruadgjer; in Spain Rogerio; and in Italy Rogero and Ruggiero. According to Miss Yonge the name signifies "spear of fame;"* it had been originally granted in meed of renown—in reward of heroism. The name became pre-eminently Norman.†

Rolf, Rollo, or Rou, a Danish sea-king, founded the Norman dynasty at Rouen, to which place he gave name, and where he reigned sixteen years (A.D. 927 to 943). He was progenitor of William the Conqueror, and of that illustrious race who have since the Conquest borne the English sceptre. During the century following the reign of Rolf at Rouen we find Roger de Toesny, who claimed descent from Malahulc, uncle of Rolf, fighting valiantly against the infidels in Spain, and achieving great victories, not without cruelty and violence. Roger married the daughter of the widowed Countess of Barcelona, "a princess," remarks Mr. Freeman, "whose dominions were practically Spanish, though her formal allegiance was due to the Parisian king. This marriage," Mr. Freeman adds, "was doubtless designed as the beginning of a Norman

---

* "History of Christian Names," by the author of "The Heir of Redclyffe." Lond.: 1863, vol. ii., p. 36.

† Out of the List compiled by M. Leopold Delisle of the Companions of William the Conqueror (*Herald and Genealogist*, vol. for 1863), no fewer than twenty-seven bear the Christian name of "Roger."

principality in Spain, but the scheme failed to take any lasting root."* On his return from Spain, Roger de Toesny rebelled against William, the future Conqueror, and sent his son, Roger de Bellomont or Beaumont against him. A battle ensued, in which Roger de Toesny and his two sons were slain.†

The latter portion of Mr. Freeman's narrative differs from other accounts of the Beaumont family. According to some Norman writers Roger à la Barbe gave name to the little town of Beaumont le Roger, beautifully situated on the Rille in Normandy. Above this town rises a limestone hill, richly wooded, at the base of which is a fountain named *La Fontaine Roger*. The latter is mentioned in the *dotalitium*, or deed of dower of Countess Judith, wife of Richard, second Duke of Normandy, who bestowed the domain on the Abbey of Bernay, from which it passed into the possession of Humphrey, Seigneur of Vieilles; which was the head place of the fief till 1040. Roger à la Barbe ‡ was the son of Humphrey; he built the castle on the summit of the rocky eminence, and his Christian name thereafter became the family designation of his House. Beaumont le Roger was besieged and captured by Henry I., afterwards by Richard Cœur de Lion; it was stormed and burned by Philip Augustus, and more than once was made an appanage of the Royal Family of France. Given to Charles the bad, King of Navarre, it was captured by Bertrand du Guesclin, and demolished. Pillaged by Henry V. in 1417, it was in 1651 ceded to the Duke of Bouillon in exchange for the principality of Sedan.§ Roger à la Barbe was one of the Conqueror's chief nobles, and his best counsellor and friend. When William left Normandy to conquer England, he associated Roger with Matilda, his queen, in the government of his kingdom. Roger helped to plan the expedition, and furnished no fewer than sixty ships for transporting the Norman army. He married in 1045 the heiress of the Count of Mulan through whom he obtained high power in France as well as in his own kingdom.

---

* Freeman's "Norman Conquest," vol. i., pp. 460–461.

† Freeman's "Norman Conquest, vol. ii. p., 197. See also sheet pedigree prefixed to the Lives of the Lindsays for some information regarding the De Toesnys.

‡ In his "Nobiliaire de Normandie," 1666, folio, M. Jacques Louis Chevillard has presented the armorial escutcheon of Roger du Mont Boumonville. The shield is *argent*, on a fesse *sable* three roses of the field; in base three lions rampant of second two and one; all within a bordure *gules*.

§ "Normandy, its History and Antiquities." Lond.

Robert de Bellomont was one of the sons of Roger à la Barbe; he is described as grandson of Turolf of Pont Andemare, by Wevia, sister of Gunnora, wife of Richard, first of that name, Duke of Normandy, great-grandfather to William I. He accompanied the Conqueror into England, and mainly contributed to the triumph at Hastings. Robert inherited the Earldom of Mellent in Normandy from his mother Adelina, daughter of Waleran, and sister of Hugh, who took the habit of a monk in the Abbey of Bec, both Earls of Mellent. Of the conduct of Robert de Bellomont at Hastings, William Pictaviensis writes :—" A certain Norman young soldier, son of Roger de Bellomont, nephew and heir to Hugh Earl of Mellent, by Adelina his sister, making the first onset in that fight, did what deserveth lasting fame, boldly charging and breaking in upon the enemy with that regiment which he commanded in the right wing of the army," for which gallant services he obtained sixty-four Lordships in Warwickshire, sixteen in Leicestershire, and one in Gloucestershire, in all ninety-one. He did not, however, attain the dignity of the English peerage before the reign of Henry I., when that monarch created him Earl of Leicester.*

Besides Robert de Bellomont, founder of the noble House of Leicester, another member of the Beaumont family took part in the Norman Conquest of England. His name of Rougere, or Fitz Roger, is entered on the roll of Battel Abbey.† Of this person, or his son, we have obtained some particulars in the *Chartulaire de la Basse-Normandie,* and also in a collection of documents relating to Normandy, transcribed from the Norman archives, and deposited in the Public Record Office. To a Latin instrument dated 1076, setting forth the independence of the church of St. Leonard against the pretensions of the Bishop of Sieux Count Roger and Roger de Bellomont appended their names, along with William the Conqueror, Matilda, his queen, and other notable persons. The instrument is as follows :—

" Quia memoria hominum sicut homines cito pertransit quedam facta eorum que cum necesse est scribendo retineri unde nos huic ecclesie providentes quod volumus successores nostros rescire, Carte huic decrevimus inserere; Contigit itaque cuidam festivitati Sᵃ Leonardi Comitem Rogerium interesse et cum eo nonnullos utriusque ordinis non mediocris fame quos ipse invitaverat ad sui honorem et huic ecclesie exaltationem. Ex quibus Sagunsin pontifex Robertus

---

* Dugdale's "Baronage," vol. i., p. 83.   † Lower's "English Surnames."

ea die nostro et comite hortante Missam cantavit *cujus etiam misse offerturam, Sibi per cupiditatem retineret emptavit. Quod nos videntes et velut monstrum exhorrentes a quodam ejus clerico, cui eam reservandam commiserat, Vi et non sine contumelia offerturam illam recessimus. Iratus propter hoc Episcopus Ecclesiam et nos excommunicare se dixit.* Quo facto prius clamorem quam fecit comes Rogerus de Sapiensi episcopo ad Johannem Rothomd Archiepiscopum die constituta ex inde placidaturi devenerimus Rothomag. Ibi in palatio et in presentio Regis et Regine Anglorum Comes Rogerus conquestus est super sagiensi episcopo qui ecclesiam S^a Leonardi sine causa excommunicare presumpsisset. At contra Episcopus nos inculpabat quod manum quam sanam et integram habuisset habendo offerturas per totum episcopatum suum. Nos ei accidissemus auferendo ab eo nostram offerturam. Ad hec Rex et Regina sertati sunt a Comite Rogero de statu ipsius ecclesie, comes vero et nos qui aderamus dilucide enarravimus quomodo Guillelmo de Bellissimo supradictam ecclesiam de peccatorum suorum veniam edificasset et quomodo eam ex precepto beate memorie pape Leonis Liberam et solutam fecisset et quod a die dedicationis ejusdem, Archiepiscopus sive episcopus nullam in ea consuetudinem habuisset nec eam ullomodo excommunicare potuisset. Aseruerunt etiam antiquissimi homines qui hoc viderant et audierant, parati probare secundum judicium Regis quod nos edisseramus. His auditis Rex et Regina jusserunt Johannem archiepiscopum et Rogerum de Bello-monte et plures alios Barones ut secundum quod audierunt facerent inde judicium. Et illi abito consilio judicaverunt ecclesiam qui tanta auctoritate et tot tanta cunque procerum confirmatione liberata esset et tam longo tempore in liberalitate perseverasset debere deinceps in perpetuum sit permanere. Episcopum injuriam fecisse, non solum Comiti Rogerio verum etiam Regi de quo ipse ecclesiam tenebat. Dixit etiam Johannes archiepiscopus quasdam ecclesias in diocesi sua esse in quibus ipse nullam omnino consuetudinem haberet. Hoc pacto, sagiensis episcopus Robertus emendavit rutum faciendo regi et comiti Rogerio injuriam quam eis fecerat predictam ecclesiam invadendo. Disfinitum est etiam ibi ut si archiepiscopus sive episcopus eam amplius inquietare presumeret apostolica et regia auctoritate a consortio fidelium usque ad satisfactionem alienus existeret. Hoc viderunt Guillielmus Rex, et Mathilda Regina, Johannis Rothomagensis archiepiscopus, Robertus sagiensis episcopus comes. Rogerius Robertus de Belism

Rogerus de Bello-monte Curvisus, Guillielmus et Hascuinus canonici
Arnellandus et multi alii."*

Translation.

Because the memory of men, like the men themselves, quickly
passes away, there are some things which ought to be committed to
writing. We, therefore, taking provident care for the future interests
of this church, have thought it right to record in this document an
event which we are desirous that our successors should be made
acquainted with. It happened then, on a certain festival of St.
Leonard, that Count (Earl) Roger was present, with some eminent
persons of both orders, whom he had invited out of respect to himself and to do honour to this church. At the joint request of ourselves and the Count, the Bishop of Sieux sang mass, and coveting
the offerings, tried to appropriate them. Observing which, and hor-
rified at it as something monstrous, we forcibly, and with reproaches,
seized them from the person—one of his clergy—to whose keeping
he had intrusted them. Enraged at this, he declared he would
excommunicate both us and our church. He fulfilled his threat, and
before Count Roger could complain of the bishop's proceedings to
the Archbishop of Rouen, we, in order to smooth matters, betook
ourselves on a set day to Rouen, and there, in the palace and in the
presence of the King and Queen of England, Count Robert charged
the Bishop of Sieux of having without just cause presumed to excommunicate the church of St. Leonard. The bishop retorted that we were
to blame, as he had a clear and legal right to all the offerings collected
in his diocese, and that we had done him a wrong by taking from
him ours. On this the king and queen conferred with Count Roger
on the state of his church, when he, together with those present,
clearly narrated how that William de Bellasis had built the aforesaid
church for the remission of his sins, and how that by an order of
Pope Leo of blessed memory it had been constituted free and inde-
pendent, and that from the day of its dedication neither archbishop
nor bishop had any customary right in it, nor in any way over it, the
power of excommunication. They asserted, moreover, that very old
men who had seen and heard all this were ready to corroborate these

* "Chartulaire de la Basse-Normandie," vol. i. p. 49, vol. i. p. 80. (Plaids
royaux vers l'année 1076. Archives d'Alençon.)

statements to the satisfaction of the king's judgment. Hearing this, the king and queen gave orders that John, the archbishop, Roger de Bellomont, and many other barons should give sentence according to the evidence. And they, counsel taken, judge that a church of such high authority, and with rights conferred by so many illustrious ancestors, had been free, and that having enjoyed its liberty for so long a time, it ought to enjoy it in perpetuity,—that the bishop had not only done an injury to Count Roger, but also to the king, of whom he held the church. John, the archbishop, further said that there were some churches in his own diocese in which he had no rights at all. Accordingly Robert, Bishop of Sieux, had to atone for the crime with which he was chargeable against the king and Count Roger in invading the privileges of the aforesaid church. It was also there decreed that if either archbishop or bishop should hereafter presume to disturb it, he should by apostolical and royal authority be separated from the communion of the faithful till such time as he had made satisfaction. This have approved William, King, and Matilda, Queen ; John, Archbishop of Rouen ; Robert, Bishop of Sieux ; Count Roger ; Robert de Bellasis ; Roger de Bellomont ; Curvisus, William, and Hascuin, canons; with Arnelland, and many others.

Roger, son of Thorold, or Torold, is celebrated in the following document, preserved in the archives of Normandy.*

" Donatio pro Sancta Trinitate rothomagensi, annuente Willelm rege Anglorum.

" Rogerius Turoldi filius ultramonte cum Willelmo comite navigaturus tres jugeres terræ in Sothevilla pro remedio animæ suæ mona- chis Sanctæ Trinitatis rotomagensis *in allodium* condonavit, sed quia in eadem navigatione morte preventus hoc confirmare nonvaluit quidam ejus miles nomine Willelmus Trenchefoil ipsum beneficium ejus vice largitus est libentissime, id ipsum Willelmo rege anglorum annuente. + Signum Willelmi regis. + S Willelmi Trenchefoil. + S bernardi forestarii. Testes Ricardus osbernus Rogerus pont + ."

Translation.

Donation to the (house of the) Holy Trinity of Rouen, by permission of William, King of England.

* See " Transcripts of Charters and other Documents, from various Archives of Normandy," in the Public Record Office, London.

Roger, son of Torold, about to travel with Count William to parts beyond the mountains, gave for the health of his soul three acres of land in Southvill to the monks of the Holy Trinity of Rouen, reserving no feudal rights, but dying on the passage, and being thereby prevented from confirming his grant, it was graciously confirmed in his stead by one William Trenchefoil, knight in his train, William, King of the English, assenting. ✠ The seal of King William, ✠ the seal of Willlam Trenchefoil, ✠ the seal of Bernard the Forester.

Witnesses, Richard Osbern and Roger the bishop ✠.

Immediately after the Norman Conquest persons of the name of Roger (members of the House of Beaumont) began to spread rapidly over England. Roger, Archdeacon of Shrewsbury (Rogerus, Archid de Salopesber), is between the years 1162 and 1182 witness to a legal instrument.* In a Pipe Roll of the sixth year of the reign of King John (1204-5), Robert de Kent, on behalf of Robert the son of Roger, renders an account of £240 18s. 4d. as dues on farming the king's rents in the county of Northumberland. In the same Roll, Robert, the son of Roger, is named as paying rent for the castle of Tynemouth.†

Among the ecclesiastics connected with the Priory of Tywardreth, Cornwall, founded soon after the Conquest, and which was a cell of the Benedictine abbey at Angers, were two priors named Roger, whose anniversaries were observed on the 12th and 31st October.‡ It may be remarked that these are the first persons of the name in a district in which members of the family are now so numerous that the late Dr. Phillpotts, Bishop of Exeter, used to indulge the jest that his diocese consisted of men, women, and Rogers's. From this early period persons bearing the name of Roger were extensively connected with the Church. Roger, styled _de Pont l'Evéque_ in Normandy,§ was Archbishop of York, 1154—1181. An ambitious churchman, his career is intimately bound up with the civil and ecclesiastical history of the kingdom. A native of Bromley in Kent,‖ he first appears under public notice in the family or court of Theobald, Arch-

---

* "Collectanea Genealogica," vol. iv. p. 15.

† Pipe Roll, in Public Record Office.

‡ "Collectanea Genealogica," vol. iii.

§ "Fasti Eboracenses," by the Rev. W. H. Dixon, edited by the Rev. James Raine. London, 1863. 8vo., vol. i., p. 233.

‖ See _postea._

bishop of Canterbury. Here he had among his companions a young priest, who was subsequently to become his rival,—the celebrated Thomas à Becket.* When Henry II. determined that his eldest son Henry should be crowned during his lifetime, he requested Archbishop Roger to perform the ceremony, owing to his quarrel with Becket, who, as Primate, was entitled to the honour. Becket hastened to anathematise Roger and two of the chief prelates who assisted him, an event which led to Becket's assassination by those who sought to vindicate the rights of the Northern province.† It is proper to add, that Roger of York proved that he was not accessory to the murder of his rival. He possessed no small share of military ardour. In 1174 he took a prominent part in the wars of the North ; he welcomed the barons who proceeded against William the Lion, and to Henry II. sent intelligence of his capture.‡ For his military zeal, Henry, in 1177, bestowed on him the castles of Scarborough and Roxburgh.§ Bishop Roger of St. Andrews, 1188—1202, was second son of Robert, third Earl of Leicester, and cousin to King William of Scotland, who made him first his Chancellor, then Abbot of Melrose, and afterwards Bishop of St. Andrews. He founded the Castle of St. Andrews as a residence for himself and his successors.‖ From 1199 till 1201 he resided chiefly in England, his name often occurring during these years as a witness to charters granted by King John to various public bodies.¶

We have thus found the Norman name of Roger travelling northward. Its *establishment* as a surname in northern parts next claims attention. Prior to his accession to the Scottish throne in 1124, David, Earl of Huntingdon, resided in England. There he married Matilda, heiress of Waltheof, Earl of Northumberland, procuring through this alliance estates in Northumberland, Cumberland, and Huntingdon. On his accession he introduced to important offices in his kingdom persons of English or Norman extraction, with whom he had associated during his sojourn in the south. Among these was Hugh de Morville, whom he constituted Constable of

* " Fasti Eboracenses," vol. i., p. 233.
† Dean Stanley's " Historical Memorials of Westminster Abbey," pp. 52-3.
‡ " Chronique de Jordan Fantosme," ed. Surtees Society, pp. 78-9, 91, 93.
§ Hoveden, 323 b; Benedict Patrib., 203.
‖ Wyntoun's " Chronicle," *passim*.
¶ Rotuli Chartarum in turri Londinensi.

Scotland. He was son of Roger de Morville and grandson of Simon
de Morville, who possessed the barony of Burgh-on-the-Sands, in
Cumberland.* Richard, a younger brother of Simon de Morville,
took part with the King of Scotland and Robert, Earl of Leicester
in the hostilities carried on against Henry II. by the young king.†

In addition to the high office of Constable with power to lead the
king's army, Hugh de Morville received extensive estates in Tweed-
dale, Lauderdale, and the Lothians, in the south-east, and in Clydes-
dale and Ayrshire in the south-west, of Scotland. He married Beatrix
Beauchamp (de Campo Bello), daughter of a powerful family of
Norman settlers in Scotland, and the reputed founders of the ducal
House of Argyle. By this marriage was born a son, Richard de
Morville, who became principal Minister of State to William the Lion.‡

Hugh de Morville resembled his royal patron, David I., in religious
devotedness. He founded the Abbey of Kilwinning in Ayrshire,
and the Abbey of Dryburgh in the county of Roxburgh. At the
period of the latter foundation (1150) we are first introduced to the
name of Roger on Scottish soil. In the Register of Dryburgh (Liber
S. Marie de Dryburgh) occur numerous entries in reference to the
acquisition of lands by Richard de Morville from Roger "Janitore
de Rogesburgh" (Roxburgh). In the foundation charter granted by
David I. we have these words :—

"Dedi dictis fratribus et eis confirmavi illam terram et omnia ad
eam pertinentia quam Beatrix de Bello Campo de Rogero Janitore
emit et iis in liberam et perpetuam elemosinam dedit. Et illud etiam
toftum extra portam occidentalem de Rogesburghe quod Johannis
Capellani fuit ita liberum et quietum iis concedo sicut carta Henrici
Comitis filii mei iis donat et confirmat."

Translation.

"I have granted and confirmed to the aforesaid brothers that land
and all its appurtenances which Beatrix de Beauchamp bought of

* "The Morvilles represented a House which had assumed its surname from the
village of Morville, on the bank of the Aire, in Picardy. The race gradually in-
creased in position and opulence; a descendant of the House in the female line
occupied for a time the Scottish throne. That descendant was John Baliol."
(Anderson's "Scottish Nation," vol. iii., pp. 730-1.)

† Dugdale.

‡ Chalmers's "Caledonia," vol. i., pp. 503-4. Anderson's "Scottish Nation,"
vol. iii., p. 731.

Roger the Janitor, and gave to them as a free and perpetual benefac-
tion. And also that parcel of land situate without the western gate
of Roxburgh, which was the property of John the Chaplain, I
yield up to them in the same free and quiet possession, as it is given
and confirmed in the charter of my son Earl Henry."

According to Du Cange, the Janitor of a Religious House held
the first grade in the ecclesiastical order; he was custodier of the
keys, and had power to reject the entrance of all who were unworthy.
Roger, "Janitor de Rogesburgh," was a landowner of considerable
extent; and therefore, independently of his ecclesiastical position, a
person of consequence. His name clearly implies his Norman or
English descent, while his transactions with Beatrix de Beauchamp,
mother of Richard de Morville, before the construction of Dryburgh
Abbey, would imply that he was a person of considerable age at the
period of the Abbey's foundation. He bore the same name as the
father of Hugh de Morville; and the first Abbot of Dryburgh, who was
nominated by Hugh, was a churchman named Roger. The coin-
cidence is sufficiently singular; but it would be rash on account
of it to assume that Roger, the Janitor, was a relative of the De
Morvilles, or that the Janitor of Roxburgh Church was subsequently
Abbot of Dryburgh Abbey.

Abbot Roger of Dryburgh took office on the 13th December,
1152.* During his incumbency he received three bulls from Pope
Alexander III., confirming grants to the Abbey, and there permitting
service during a general interdict. He resigned his office as Abbot
in 1177; and proceeded to England probably under the patronage of
Archbishop Roger of York, who was, like himself, a favourite of
Alexander III., the reigning Pope.

Members of the Roger family held offices in the Religious Houses
of the Scottish and English Border from the twelfth century down-
ward. On the 29th April, 1217, Roger, Master of the Lay Brothers
of the Abbey of Warden in Northumberland, was elected Lord
Abbot of Rieuall, or Rievaux, in Yorkshire; he afterwards demitted
his office, and was succeeded by Leo, Abbot of Dundrennan, and
Monk of Melrose.†

In 1236 "Dominus Rogerus Cellerarius" was translated from

---

* Liber S. Marie de Dryburgh.
† Chronica de Mailros.

Melrose to the Abbey of Neubothel (Newbottle).* Abbot Roger
of Newbottle assisted at the conference which took place at Roxburgh between Henry III. of England and Alexander III. of
Scotland, on the 20th September, 1255. He attended a chapter
of his order held in England, and on his return towards Scotland,
died at the Monastery of Vandy in 1256.† A second Abbot of
Dryburgh was also a member of the Roger family. " Rogerus, Abbas
de Dryburgh" is witness to a charter along with William de Lamber-
ton, Bishop of St. Andrews, whose episcopate extended from 1298
to 1328.‡

Before proceeding further it is essential that we make some
observations respecting the origin of surnames. According to Du
Chesne, the lords of France began to assume the names of their
demesnes so early as the year 989. Camden relates that surnames
were commenced in England under Edward the Confessor. Be this
as it may, it is certain that a great impulse to the use of surnames
was given by the Norman adventurers, many of whom assumed as
family designations the names of *Chateaux*, or Villages, on the other
side of the Channel. At the Domesday Valuation surnames were
not uncommon ; they were frequent among persons of rank in
England in the middle of the twelfth century.§ In Scotland they
were not common till half a century later. Ordinary persons took
names from their calling or trades, or from the aspects of their
localities ;‖ but those who possessed Norman blood always preferred
as surnames the designations of their ancestral homes, or their own
Christian names.

Early in the fourteenth century flourished in or near the town
of Roxburgh a landowner known as " Roger of Auldton." Surnames were now in universal use, and Roger had doubtless been for
some time the family designation of the owner of the *auld toon*, or
old town, of Roxburgh. The " old town " of Melrose in Roxburghshire still exists, likewise the al-ton, or old town, of Aberdeen. An
ancestor of Roger of Auldton had doubtless built the original place or

* Registrum S. Marie de Neubotle, 1140—1528. Edinb. 1849, 4ᵗᵒ, p. 154.
† Chronica de Mailros.
‡ Chalmers's "Caledonia," *passim.*
§ An Essay on Family Nomenclature by Mark Antony Lower. Lond., 1849,
12mo., vol. I. p. 31.
‖ Inquisitiones Nonarum, 1340 (13th Edward III.)

village of Roxburgh—hence the designation of his descendant. It is, indeed, not improbable that the original settler—probably Roger the Janitor—gave name to the entire province. The old name of Roxburgh was Marken.* In charters of the reign of David I. it is designated "Rogysburgh"—which is precisely the pronunciation that would now be given by Scottish Borderers to the word Rogers-burgh.† We offer the conjecture as a probable solution of an etymological difficulty.‡

In 1328, Robert de Colvil "Lord of Oxenham quitclaimed to Roger of Auldton, near Roxburgh, an annual revenue of five shillings in which he was bound to him for two oxgangs of land, which he held of him in the town and territory of Heton, granting also to the said Roger the liberty of converting the said two oxgangs to pious uses or perpetual alms."§ During the same year Roger of Auldton obtained a "quitclaim" from John de Valays, whereby he was freed from an annual payment of "two pence yearly for two oxgangs of land" which Roger's father, Gilbert, had undertaken to pay to Henry, father of John."‖ With lands at Auldton of Roxburgh Roger proceeded in 1329 to endow "a chantry of one priest, who should ever after perform Divine service in Saint James's church, Roxburgh."¶ For endowment he granted "all his lands, revenues

* Holinshead's "Scottish Chronicle," Arbroath, 1805, vol. i, p. 1367.

† "Origines Parochiales," vol. i., *passim*.

‡ There has been considerable discussion among antiquaries as to the origin of the name Roxburgh. Some maintain that it is a corruption of Rose-burgh, a place of primroses ; others, that Roch, a saint, had his cell in the locality ; others, that being the head-quarters of Border thieves, it was at first styled Rogues-burgh. In confirmation of our own theory, it may be remarked that the name of Roger was common among the old landowners of the south-eastern Border. In a Jury summoned by Alexander III. in 1262 for determining a dispute between the burgesses of Peebles and the laird of Crockston relative to the digging of peat, occur the names of Roger of Kedistun, and Roger, the gardener. In the Ragman Rolls (1291—1296) are inserted in connection with the south-eastern district, the names of Roger le Mareschal, and Rogier de Mohaut (W. Chambers's "History of Peeblesshire."—Edin., 8vo., 1864, pp. 50, 64). A place near Lauder, which belonged to Dryburgh Abbey, was known as Roger's Law (Liber S. Marie de Dryburgh, p. 325). There is a Roger's Crag near Halmyre, in Peeblesshire, (Chambers's "Peeblesshire," p. 43).

§ Liber de Calchou ; Register of Kelso, pp. 369, 370. *Origines Parochiales Scotiæ*, vol. i., *passim*.

‖ Origines Parochiales, vol. i, pp. 452—460.

¶ Liber de Calchou, p. 368 ; Regist. Glasg., p. 244.

and possessions in the town and territory of Auldton, together with the whole demesnes which he held in the said territory." This grant was confirmed by charters from King Robert the Bruce and the Bishop of Glasgow ; and Margaret, wife of the donor, to indicate her approval, made an addition to the grant and stipulated that, "forty pounds of silver should be paid to the fabric of the cathedral church of Glasgow" if she or her heirs should revoke it. The entire annual endowments provided for the chantry by Roger of Auldton and his wife amounted to £20 Scots, or about £200 of present money.[*]

Long as they had been settled in Scotland, the members of the House of Roger remembered whence they had sprung. In 1360 the church of Old Roxburgh was granted by Edward I. to Roger of Bromley.[†] From Bromley (county of Kent) came Archbishop Roger, of York, the close ally of Roger de Morville, whose son Hugh is said to have avenged his quarrel with Thomas à Becket. At Bromley the House of Roger was planted in the time of the Conqueror, and there members of the family continued to live prosperously for centuries. At least one family of the name is still resident in the locality.[‡] In a sasine of the burgh of Berwick dated 1291-2, Roger is named as Keeper (Custos) under Edward I.[§] In the counties of Roxburgh, Berwick, and Selkirk, persons of the name are occasionally to be found. But the main branch of the House migrated westward. The period and circumstances of that migration we shall now endeavour to determine.

In his "History of Ayrshire and its Families," Mr. James Paterson writes,[||] "During the reign of Robert the Bruce, and before 1321, Eustacia de Colvil, relict of Sir Reginald le Chene, and daughter and heiress of Sir William Colvil of Ochiltree,[¶] granted to the monks of Melrose the church and church-lands of Ochiltree ; and the grant was confirmed by a charter of Robert de Colvil of Oxnam and Ochiltree. This Robert de Colvil of Oxnam is the same who, as 'Lord of Oxen-

* "Origines Parochiales," vol. i., pp. 452—460.
† "Rotuli Scotiæ," vol. i., p. 852. "Origines Parochiales," vol. i., p. 453.
‡ To Colonel Joseph L. Chester, author of the "Life of John Rogers, the first Martyr of the English Reformation," we are indebted for copious extracts from the parish register of Bromley in connection with the Roger family from 1582 to 1666.
§ "Chronica de Mailros."
|| Paterson's "History of Ayrshire," vol. ii., p. 394.
¶ Liber de Melrose, p. 343.

ham,' quitclaimed in 1328 to Roger of Auldton an annual revenue of five shillings for lands in the town and territory of Heton." He held lands both in Roxburghshire and Ayrshire, having probably succeeded to the territory of the Morvilles in those counties. At the period when he granted lands at Ochiltree to Melrose Abbey, the head of that establishment was Abbot Roger,* a member, no doubt, of the church-loving family of Auldton. Probably through his recommendation Robert de Colvil, as a good son of the Church, made the quit claim to Roger of Auldton of his feu-rent of the lands at Heton ; and it is not unreasonable to conclude that the same generous churchman planted some of his kindred on the newly-acquired church lands at Ochiltree, where they were found long afterwards. It was a practice of churchmen to serve their near relations by providing them with farms on easy terms on their church lands. To the Abbey of Dryburgh, and Roger, its first abbot, David I. granted a manor at Carail (Crail),† Fifeshire, and there the patronymic of Roger has remained till recent times.‡

The church lands of Ochiltree were retained by the monks of Melrose till the period of the Reformation,§ and so long did the Roger family find headquarters in that Ayrshire parish. In the first volume of the Commisariat Register of Glasgow is recorded the will of Alexander Roger in Ochiltree, made in 1549 or 1550. From the inventory of his goods he appears to have been a substantial farmer. The inventory includes "one horse, three mares, four oxen, eight cows, two stirks (young bullocks), nineteen sheep, forty bolls of oats, five and a half bolls of barley, and household goods to the value of fifty pounds." In his will he bequeaths *fourpence* "to the building of St. Kentigern." Between 1153 and 1160 Malcolm IV. granted " to the church of St. Kentigern, Glasgow, and to Bishop Herbert and his successors, the

---

* Lord Blachford of Wisdome, formerly Sir Frederick Rogers, Bart., a representative of the Roger family in England, is married to a daughter of Mr. Colvile of Ochiltree, whose progenitor granted to the monks of Melrose his lands of Ochiltree, thereby affording a home and headquarters to a family, a member of which has, after five centuries, become allied in marriage to an ennobled descendant of the sept.

† Liber S. Marie de Dryburgh.

‡ Baptismal Registers of Crail, and of the adjacent parishes of Kingsbarns and Anstruther.

§ Paterson's " Ayrshire," vol. ii., p. 394.

church of Old Rokesburgh, with all its appurtenances." * And in virtue of this connection between the church of Old Roxburgh and the cathedral of St. Kentigern at Glasgow, we find Margaret, wife of Roger of Auldton, stipulating, in 1329, that the sum of forty pounds of silver should be paid to the fabric of the cathedral if she or her heirs should revoke her supplementary grant to the chantry of St. James's Church, Roxburgh.† So in after generations did Alexander Roger, as a faithful son of the Church, and a descendant of the pious laird of Auldton, feel called on to remember the fabric of St. Kentigern.‡

A member of the House of Roger was a distinguished pioneer of the Scottish Reformation, and one of its martyrs. He is thus described by John Knox :—"Johne Roger, a Blake Freir, godly, learned, and ane that had fructfully preached Christ Jesus to the comforte of many in Anguss and Mearnes, whom that bloody man (Cardinal Beaton) caused murther in the ground of the Sea-toure of Sanctandross, and then caused to cast him ower the craig, sparsing a fals bruyt (report) that the said Johnne seeking to flie had broken his awin craig."§ John Roger suffered in 1544, eleven years prior to the martyrdom of his namesake and remote relative John Rogers, the English proto-martyr, who was burned at Smithfield on the 4th February, 1555. He was in all probability a member of the Black-friars Monastery at Dundee, whence the report of his preaching would readily reach Cardinal Beaton at St. Andrews, a town distant from Dundee eleven Scottish miles.

Andrew Stewart, third Lord Ochiltree, usually styled "The good Lord," was a zealous promoter of the Reformation. His daughter, Margaret Stewart, became second wife of John Knox ; the marriage took place in March, 1564, when the Reformer was in his fifty-eighth year. "The good Lord" was probably enlightened in the reformed doctrines by the converted Black Friar, who, we have no doubt was a scion of the family of Roger at Ochiltree, and was born on the estate.

* Regist. Glasg., p. 14.

† See *ante*.

‡ In his Testament, 12th July, 1547, Allan Stewart, in Allanton, bequeaths " 4 pennies to the fabric of S. Kentigern." Among his creditors is " Alexander Roger," to the amount of 6s.

§ John Knox's " Works," edited by David Laing, LL.D., vol. i., p. 119.

The Reformation proved a temporal benefit to the great Reformer's brother-in-law. Between 1570 and 1592 Lord Ochiltree received four charters under the Great Seal of lands and baronies at Ochiltree, including the church lands of the Parish.* The transference of the tenure led to the exodus from the church lands of the old tenants—the Rogers, whom we must now trace in other scenes.

On the 24th May, 1581, David Roger in Redie,† parish of Airlie, Forfarshire, executed his will. In this document he names Lord Saltoun as his landlord ("maister of the grund") at Airlie, and expresses himself as indebted to Lord Ochiltree in "teind-beir." All Lord Ochiltree's lands were situated at Ochiltree and in the adjoining parishes. David Roger evidently hailed from thence, and as payee of "teind" or feu-duty on his ancestral acres was, it is presumed, head of the House. The Rogers at Redie were persons of considerable substance. David Roger died on the 26th February, 1582. By his will he constituted his elder son William his sole executor, and, excepting "200 merks" to his younger son David, endowed him with his "haill guidis." William Roger died in February, 1589—his free substance at his decease amounting to £1,456 Scots. To his son John he bequeathed the lease of his farm, but his son James appears to have obtained the principal portion of his estate. In 1606 the latter executed a settlement of his affairs, in which he specifies that should his sons die before succeeding him in his "rowme," or inheritance, his daughters should be permitted to enjoy the succession, only on the condition that should they marry, their husbands should bear the surname of Roger.‡ James Roger determined to establish a Family, but he did not succeed. Members of the Roger Family remained at Airlie till the beginning of the present century, when they became extinct in the male line.§

Among the members of the Roger Family who left Ochiltree was William Roger, who died in 1562, tenant-farmer at Coupar Grange, parish of Bendochy, Perthshire. This individual paid rent to the Cistercian Abbey of Coupar of £22 11s. 10d. Scots. At the time of his decease his personal estate amounted to £432 18s. 6d. Scots, exclusive of "silver lent to the laird of Ruthven"—probably his

---

* Paterson's "Ayrshire Families."
† Commissariat Record of Edinburgh.
‡ Edinburgh Commissariat Register, 1610.
§ Marriage and Baptismal Registers of Airlie.

wife's dowry. His will, with the corresponding inventory, is a document of sufficient interest to be presented entire. It is as follows :—*

"The Testament testamentar and Inventar of the guidis geir soumis of money and debtis pertaining to umquhil William Roger, in Couper Grange in Angus the tyme of his decease, quha deceasit in the month of Junij the year of God 1562 years faithfully maid and given up by himself as containing the nomination of executors and inventory of his guidis and partlie maid and given up by Marjorie Blair his relict and William Roger his sone as containing the debtis awand to him and be him quhome he nominat his Executors in his latter Will underwritten, of the daitt at Couper Grange the 16th day of Apryll the year of God foresaid before thir witnesses Alexander Cumming, George Ewen, William Quhittsoun, John Quhittsoun his neibouris with utheris diverse.

" In the first the said umquhil William Roger had the guidis geir soumis of money and debtis of the avail and prices after following perteyning to him at the tyme of his decease foresaid, viz. 8 oxin, price of the peece 6 lib summa 48 lib. Item 3 ky, price of the peece 4 lib summa 12 lib. Item ane horse, twa meres ane foall by the heirezeld horse,† price of them 16 lib. Item 9 stottis and queyis, twa and three years auld, price of the peece oure heide 4 merkis, summa 24 lib; 6 auld scheip price of the peece 13s. 4d. summa 4 lib; Item 24 hoggis price of the peece 6s. 8d. summa 8 lib. Item sawin on the ground 40 bollis aittis, estimat to the third corne extending to 6 score bollis aittis, price of the boll with the fodder 20s., summa 120 lib. Item mair 15 bollis beir sawin estimat to the fird (fourth) corne extending to sixty bollis beir price of the bolle with the fodder 30s. summa 90 lib; Item in peis 58 lib money. Item in utensils and domicilis with the abulzements of his bodye estimat to three score pundis. Summa of the Inventar 440 lib.

" Followis the debtis awand to the deid. Item, there wes awand to the said umquhil William Roger be William Quhittsoun in Couper Grange 20 merkis—Item Mair be him 6 libs for whilk he is actit in the officials bookis of Dunkeld.

" Item be John Guthrie 42s.

" Summa of the debtis awand to the deid 20 lib 3 : 6d.

" Summa of the Inventar with the debtis 460 lib 3 : 8d.

" Followis the debtis awand be the deid.

" Item, ther wes awand be the said umquhil William Roger to the Abbey of Couper for the ferm of the grund in anno 1562 15 bollis I peck beir at 30s. the boll, summa 22 libs 11s. 10d.

" Mair 3 bollis aittis at 20s. the boll, summa 3 libs. Item Mair for the teind in anno foresaid 12 bollis victuall thereof 5 bollis beir and 7 bollis meat at 30s. the bolle over heid—summa 18 libs.

" Item, to his servants for the rest of their yearis fee and boun-tith, viz. to Johne Simpson, 30s. to Robert Spence 30s. and to Margaret Moncur 13s. 4d.

" Summa of the debtis awand to the deid 27 lib. 5s. 2d. Restis of free geir the debtis deductit 432 lib. 18s. 6d. to be dividit in three partis; the deid's part * is 144 libs 6s. 1d. whereof the quot is componed for four libs.

" Follow the Deids legacy and latter will.

" At Couper Grange the 16th day of April the yeir of God 1562 yeirs the whilk day the said William Roger made his legacy and latter will as follows :—

" I leave Executors and Intromitters my wife Marjorie Blair and my son William Roger. I mak Oversmen David Roger in Redie William Roger his son Johne Diksoune and Johne Broun to see that the Executors do that they aucht to do to the bairnis and the gudewyf als lang as she halds hir but ane man to be maister of the hale hous. The silver that is in the Laird of Ruthven's hands gif it happens to be delyverit in the gudewyf's tyme, the gudeman and the gudewyf are content that it be delyverit to the bairnis and disponit to them quha hes mister† be sight of the Oversmen. And this baith the gudeman and the gudewyf is content hereof with the advice of all the Oversmen together.

" This was done before thir witnesses Alexander Cumming, George Ewen, William Quhittsoun, John Quhittsoun, his neibouris with

* The "deid's part" is that portion of a man's movable estate which he is entitled to dispose of by testament. If a man leaves a widow and no children, the widow is entitled to one half of the free movables as her *jus relictæ*. If children are left and no widow, one half of the free movables go to the child or children as *legitim*. When both widow and children are left, the widow has a third as a *jus relictæ*, the child a third as *legitim*, and the remaining third constitutes "the dead's part," which may be disposed of by will according to inclination.
† Need.

utheris divers. Sic subscribitur, William Roger. The above Will was confirmed before the Commissary at Dunkeld on the 18th July, 1583."

At the Reformation the lands of the Cistercian Abbey of Coupar were divided into twelve portions.* One of these portions—which had constituted the farm of William Roger of "the Will"—became the property of his son William, who, by William Roger of Redie, in his will executed in 1589, is styled "portioner of Coupar-Grange." The estate was probably purchased with the sum of money which his parents had lent at interest to the Laird of Ruthven.

By the extinction of the House of Roger of Redie, elder branch of the Rogers of Ochiltree, the representation of the Family reverted to the Rogers of Coupar-Grange. William Roger, portioner of Coupar-Grange, is in 1589† styled by William Roger of Redie, his "brother-in-law;" which would imply that even a few years after the Reformation the marriage of cousins was not obnoxious or distasteful. William Roger, of Coupar-Grange, was father of two sons, William, his successor, and George. The latter proceeded to Dundee, and there engaged in merchandise and shipping. He died in 1611, aged thirty-three; his tombstone in the old burial-ground of Dundee is inscribed thus:—" Hic · dormienti · pietate · et · virtvte · insigni · viro · Georgio · Roger · Navclero · et · civi · hvivs · oppidi · qvi · obiit · anno · 1611 · die · primo · Octobris · ætatis · vero · svæ · anno · 33 · hoc · faciendvm · procvravit · eivs · conivnx · Elizabetha · Loch. malovnie · mihi · hodie · cras · tibi." By his wife, Elizabeth Loch-malonie, he left one son, William, who became a prosperous merchant at Dundee, and held office in the Magistracy. He married Euphan, daughter of James Man, merchant, maternal aunt of William Duncan, of Seaside, a progenitor of the Earls of Camperdown. Bailie William Roger mortified or bequeathed in 1659 "one half of his real and personal estate" for the education and training of seven "poor male children" within the burgh. His widow established a Merchants' Widows Fund at Dundee. William Roger, second "portioner," of Coupar-Grange, married Elspeth Angus, by whom he became father of George Roger, who was baptized on the 28th January,

* "New Statistical Account of Scotland," vol. x., p. 1190.
† Will of William Roger, of Redie, formerly quoted.

1649.* According to family tradition, William Roger died of "the Plague," a pestilent sickness which visiting this part of the country in 1664 decimated the population. His widow disposed of the family estate to a prosperous tradesman. George Roger continued to reside on the estate till his death in 1710. He married Catherine, daughter of Bisset, Baron of Bilbo,† and had issue four sons, William, Charles, James, and Patrick, and three daughters, Anne, Margaret, and Janet. Anne, the eldest daughter, born May, 1680, married John Davie, parish of Coupar-Angus, and had issue. The second daughter, Margaret, born April, 1682, married John Stewart, farmer, Greendykes, Perthshire, and had issue. Janet, the youngest daughter, baptized 19th September, 1686, married 1st April, 1709,‡ James Playfair, farmer, Couttie, parish of Bendochy,

* Baptismal Register of Bendochy.

† A small barony in Perthshire, now included in some larger possession, and the ame forgotten.

‡ John Playfair, brother of James Playfair, farmer, Couttie, rented a farm at Coupar-Grange. He married Jean Ure, and was father of four sons, Patrick, Charles, James, and John. James was baptized 25th February, 1714, studied at the University of St. Andrews, and obtained licence as a probationer of the Church, 6th September, 1739. He was ordained minister of the united parishes of Liff and Benvie, 2nd March, 1743, and died 28th May, 1772. By his marriage with Margaret Young he had seven sons, of whom five attained maturity; viz., John, Robert, William, Andrew, and James, and three daughters, Margaret and Barbara, and a daughter who died young. John, the eldest son, was born 10th March, 1748, and was educated at the University of St. Andrews. In his eighteenth year he became candidate for the Professorship of Mathematics in Marischal College, Aberdeen, and though unsuccessful, highly distinguished himself in a public competition. In 1773 he was ordained minister of Liff and Benvie, in succession to his father. In 1785 he was appointed joint Professor of Mathematics in the University of Edinburgh, a chair which he exchanged for that of Natural Philosophy in 1805. He died unmarried, 19th July, 1819. He published "Elements of Geometry," "Outlines of Natural Philosophy," and many other valuable scientific works. He is commemorated by a monument on the Calton Hill of Edinburgh.

Robert, second son of the Rev. James Playfair, of Liff and Benvie, married Margaret Macniven. Their son, William II. Playfair, was architect of Donaldson's Hospital, the New College, and other public buildings at Edinburgh. He died 18th of March, 1857.

William Playfair, a younger son of the Rev. James Playfair, of Liff and Benvie, and brother of Professor Playfair, was an ingenious mechanic, and an eminent miscellaneous writer. He was born in 1759, and died 11th February, 1823. He married, and left sons and daughters. John, youngest brother of the Rev. James

by whom she became mother of six sons, George, James, Patrick, William, Charles, and John, and five daughters, Catherine, Barbara, Margaret, Isobel, and Janet. Of the sons, James, Patrick, William, and John died unmarried.

Charles, the fourth son, baptized 26th April, 1721, rented the farm of Muirton, parish of Bendochy. He married, 3rd July, 1750, Catherine Henderson, parish of Blairgowrie, and had issue ten sons, James, George, Charles, David (died in infancy), John (died in infancy), David, John, William, Ebenezer, and Peter; and two daughters, Margaret and Catherine. Margaret, elder daughter, born December, 1768, married John Hill of Cotton, in the county of Forfar, and had issue two sons, John and David, and two daughters, Catherine and Anne. John Hill, the elder son, born 1793, succeeded his father in the estate of Cotton; he died, unmarried, in 1847. He was succeeded by his brother David, who was born in 1801, and died, unmarried, in 1860. Catherine, elder daughter, died young; Anne, younger daughter, born in 1798, married James Thomas, solicitor, Perth, and died in 1840, leaving two sons and two daughters. Catherine, younger daughter of Charles Playfair and Catherine Henderson, married John Clarke, farmer, Balbrogie, and had issue. James, the eldest son of Charles Playfair, and grandson of Janet Roger, baptized 3rd May, 1752, was licensed 6th August, 1777, and ordained minister of Bendochy, 7th February, 1791. On the 19th December, 1790, he married Grizel Duncan, by whom he had four sons, Patrick, Charles, James, and George, and a daughter, Catherine. He died 22nd April, 1812.[*]

George, eldest son of James Playfair, and Janet Roger, rented the farm of Knowhead, or West Bendochy. He married his cousin, Jean Roger (see *postea*).

——— ———

Playfair, married Catherine, daughter of John Moncur, farmer, Nether-town of Coupar-Grange, by whom he became father of two sons, Patrick and John, and of five daughters, Isabel, Grizel, Elizabeth, Jean, and Catherine.

[*] The Rev. James Playfair, minister of Bendochy, composed a large and important work on the culture and management of bees, the MS. of which was unhappily destroyed by a fire in the printing-office. The author had bestowed twenty years on its preparation, and could not be induced to make an effort towards retrieving his loss.

David, sixth son of Charles Playfair, and grandson of Janet Roger, born March, 1765, rented the farm of Hill of Couttie, parish of Bendochy; he married, and had issue. Peter, the youngest son, emigrated to the West Indies, and there died *s. p.*

Charles, second son of George Roger and Catherine Bisset, born June, 1689, married first Grizel Mackie, June, 1716, and secondly Margaret Hill, parish of Eassie, March, 1718. By his second marriage he had issue two children, John and Catherine, who both died young. James, third son of George Roger, born April, 1691, died, unmarried, 2nd December, 1706, and is commemorated by an altar tombstone in the churchyard of Bendochy. Patrick, fourth son of George Roger, born March, 1693, rented a farm at Coupar-Grange. He married, 14th August, 1718, Margaret Kidd, parish of St. Martin's, and had issue six sons, James, George, William, Thomas, Charles, and Patrick, and four daughters, Janet, Jean, Barbara, and Margaret. Janet, eldest daughter, born January, 1727, married John Blair, and had issue. James, eldest son, born November, 1719, married Margaret Corson, and had issue, Peter, born September, 1748; James, born April, 1750; Margaret, born March, 1752; and Sophia, born September, 1754. George, second son, engaged in business at Dundee, married, and had issue. William, third son, rented a farm at Tealing, married, and had issue. Charles, fifth son, a manufacturer, and Convener of the Incorporated Trades in Dundee, married, first, Grizel, eldest daughter of Thomas Davidson, of Wolflaw, and secondly Catherine Young, Dundee. By his second marriage he had issue Charles Young Roger, a daughter Catherine, and others.

William, eldest son of George Roger, was baptized 20th January, 1684. He married, first, Margaret Wright, daughter of the Laird of Lawton, near Coupar-Angus, and secondly (12th August, 1726), Janet Gellatly, parish of Lethendy. By his first marriage he had issue George, born May, 1716; Jean, born January, 1711; Janet, born June, 1714; Barbara, born March, 1718; and Sophia, born April, 1719, who died young. By his second marriage he had issue William, born June, 1727; Peter, born May, 1732; David, born February, 1735, and Sophia, born December, 1729.

Of William Roger's daughters, Jean, the eldest, married her cousin, George Playfair, farmer, Knowhead; she died at St. Andrews in 1804, aged ninety-three. She was mother of two sons,

William and James. William, baptized 7th December, 1736, died young. James, the younger son, born December, 1738, was ordained minister of Newtyle, Forfarshire, 1st November, 1770. He was translated to the neighbouring parish of Meigle, and in 1799 was appointed Principal of the United College, St. Andrews, and minister of St. Leonard's Church in that city. Principal Playfair published "Systems of Chronology and Geography" and other historical works. He was Doctor of Divinity, and Historiographer to His Royal Highness the Prince of Wales. He died 26th May, 1819. He married, 30th September, 1773, Margaret Lyon,* descended from a branch of the noble family of Strathmore (who died 4th November, 1831), and had four sons and five daughters. George, the eldest son, born 1782, became Principal Inspector-General of Hospitals, Bengal. He married Jessie Ross, and had issue (with others now deceased) George, born 1816, lately Principal of the Medical College, Agra;† Lyon, M.P. for the Universities of St. Andrews and Edinburgh; Robert Lambert, born 1828, lately Consul at Zanzibar, and now Consul-General at Algiers; William Smoult, born 1835, physician in London, and James Octavius, deceased. George Playfair died in 1845.

William Davidson Playfair, second son of Principal Playfair, and grandson of Jean Roger, born 1783, became a Colonel in the Indian Army; he married Ann Ross, and had issue thirteen sons and daughters, of whom survive *Colonel* George William, *Major* Elliot

---

* Mrs. Playfair's brother, the Rev. James Lyon, D.D., minister of Glammis (died 3rd April, 1838), married, 25th January, 1786, Agnes, daughter of John Ramsay L'Amy, of Dunkenny, Forfarshire. This lady was author of "Neil Gow's Farewell to Whisky," and other poetical compositions. She died 14th December, 1840.

† Dr. Lyon Playfair was born at Bengal in 1818. In 1843 he was appointed Professor of Chemistry in the Royal Institution, Manchester. After serving as a Sanitary Commissioner, Chemist to the Museum of Practical Geology, Joint Secretary to the Department of Science and Art, and Inspector-General of Government Museums, he was in 1858 elected Professor of Chemistry in the University of Edinburgh, and President of the Chemical Society of London. He resigned his university chair in 1869, on being elected representative in Parliament of the Universities of St. Andrews and Edinburgh. He is Ph.D. of Giessen; LL.D. of St. Andrews and Edinburgh; a Fellow of the Royal Society; and Companion of the Bath. Dr. Lyon Playfair married, in 1846, Margaret, daughter of James Oakes, of Riddings, Derbyshire; and in 1857, Jean Ann, daughter of Crowley Millington, of Crowley House, and has issue.

Minto, *Major* William, and Jessie, wife of Stuart Grace, Town Clerk, St. Andrews. Colonel W. D. Playfair died in 1852.

Lieutenant-Colonel Sir Hugh Lyon Playfair, LL.D., third son of Principal Playfair, was born in 1786. He was distinguished in India as an artillery officer, and as constructor of the great military road between Calcutta and Benares. For many years chief magistrate of St. Andrews, he found the place in decay, and effected its restoration. For his important services in India and as restorer of the city of St. Andrews he was honoured with knighthood and other distinctions. He died at St. Andrews on the 23rd January, 1861, in the 75th year of his age. He is commemorated by an elegant monument in the cathedral churchyard, St. Andrews. By his marriage with Jane Dalgleish, of Scots-craig, he had eleven children. His eldest son, William Dalgleish, lieutenant in the 33rd Regiment, Bengal Native Infantry, fell at the battle of Sobraon, 16th February, 1846, aged 25 years. His second son, Arthur, an officer in the Indian Army, also fell in one of the engagements in India. Frederick, third son, now a major in the Indian Army, married in 1855, and has issue. Archibald, fourth son, is in the Indian service. The youngest son, Henry, is resident in Glasgow. Of Sir Hugh's daughters, Margaret Adelaide, the eldest, married *Lieutenant* Charles McKechnie, 93rd Regiment, and died, leaving issue. Jane Julia, second daughter, is wife of Gregor McGregor, banker, St. Andrews. Mary, third daughter, married C. Murray, merchant, China; and Frances Makgill, fourth daughter, married William Lees, A.M.

James Playfair, youngest son of Principal Playfair, and grandson of Jean Roger, was born in 1791. He was a merchant in Glasgow, and a magistrate of that city. He was twice married, and left issue. His eldest surviving son, John, is settled as a merchant in Toronto. Another son, George, is a merchant at Glasgow. His only daughter, Margaret, is wife of the Rev. William Fraser, A.M., minister of Free St. Bernard's Church, Edinburgh. James Playfair died in 1866.

Of Principal Playfair's five daughters, Margaret, the eldest, died unmarried, August, 1810. Jean, second daughter, married Patrick Playfair, of Dalmarnock, 4th February, 1802. Janet, third daughter, married the Rev. James Macdonald; she died 20th October, 1864. Mary Lyon, fourth daughter, married, 14th May, 1808, Colonel (afterwards General) David Campbell, of Williamston, Perthshire; she died in 1810, leaving one son, James David Lyon Campbell, of Williamston, who married Alicia Richarda Houghton, and had issue four sons, Charles, Henry, George, and Arthur. The Principal's youngest daughter, Hugh Elizabeth, married Samuel Caw, merchant, Glasgow, 23rd January, 1810; issue two sons, John, deceased, and James, an eminent artist.

Barbara, third daughter of William Roger, married James Millar, farmer, Coupar-Grange, and had issue one son, George, who died *s. p.*, and four daughters, Isabella, married William Taylor, Meigle ; Jean, married John Duncan, farmer, Bothrie, died *s. p.*; Elizabeth, married Peter Crichton, farmer, Hatton, parish of Newtyle, with issue ; and Barbara, married William Gow, farmer, Coupar-Grange, with issue.

Sophia, fifth daughter of William Roger, born 1729, married, 23rd August, 1701, John Playfair, farmer, West Town of Coupar-Grange, and had issue four sons, William, born February, 1755 (died young) ; John, born 1763 ; Patrick, born September, 1765 ; James, born March, 1769 (died young); and four daughters, Anne, born February, 1753 ; Sophia, born January, 1762 (died young) ; Jean, born July, 1767 ; and Margaret, born April, 1771. Anne, the eldest daughter, married, 20th December, 1774, Thomas Myles, merchant, Perth, and had issue three sons, John, Robert, and Thomas. The two latter died unmarried. John, engaged in merchandise. He married Margaret, daughter of the Rev. Alexander Blyth, minister of the Associate Church, Kinclaven, Perthshire. and had issue. His eldest son, the Rev. Thomas Myles, minister of Aberlemno, Forfarshire, is author of "The Kernel of the Controversy," and other publications. John, the younger son, is a solicitor in Forfar. Jean, third daughter of John Playfair and Sophia Roger, married Peter Grant, Perth, and had children, who all died young. Margaret, youngest daughter of John Playfair, married Robert Davidson, farmer, Tealing, Forfarshire, and left one daughter, who married Thomas Mudie, and had issue.

John, second son of John Playfair and Sophia Roger, married Margaret Henderson. He was a merchant in Perth, and there died in 1833 without issue.

Patrick, third son of John Playfair and Sophia Roger, engaged in merchandise in Antigua, and having realized a fortune, purchased the estate of Dalmarnock, in the county of Lanark. He married, 4th February, 1802, Jean, second daughter of Principal James Playfair, of St. Andrews; she died 24th November, 1852. Patrick Playfair died 26th November, 1836; he was father of five sons and five daughters. James, the eldest son, died, unmarried, 22nd February, 1866; two sons, each named John, died young; Patrick is a merchant in Glasgow, and president of the Chamber of Commerce in that city; he married Georgiana, daughter of John Muir, merchant, Glasgow, and has issue six sons and three daughters; the youngest son is the Rev. David Playfair, B.A., Cantab., minister of Abercorn, Linlithgowshire; he married in 1854 Jane Kincaid, daughter of James Pitcairn, M.D., Edinburgh, and has issue two sons and two daughters.

Margaret, eldest daughter of Patrick Playfair, and granddaughter of Sophia Roger, married, 27th April, 1831, the Rev. Charles Jobson Lyon, minister of the Episcopal Church, St. Andrews, and author of " History of St. Andrews," 2 vols., 8vo., Edin., 1843, and has issue three sons and two daughters. Sophia, second daughter of Patrick Playfair, married, 1st October, 1834, the Rev. James Chrystal, D.D., minister of Auchinleck, with issue four sons and two daughters. Mary, third daughter of Patrick Playfair and granddaughter of Sophia Roger, married, 23rd July, 1839, the Rev. Patrick Fairbairn, D.D., now Principal of the Free Church College, Glasgow; she died 9th December, 1852, leaving two sons and two daughters. Anne and Jane Hugh, younger daughters of Patrick Playfair of Dalmarnock, are unmarried.

George Roger, son of William Roger by his first wife, Margaret Wright, died unmarried; William, second son of William Roger, and first by his second marriage, rented the farm of Coupar-Grange. He married, first, Isabella, daughter of George Constable, Bendochy, and secondly, Elizabeth, daughter of J. Robertson, Tullynydie. His two sons George and William, and his daughter Margaret, died in infancy. His surviving daughter Janet married John West, farmer, Mayriggs, parish of Bendochy, and had issue two sons.

Peter, third son of William Roger, rented the farm of Ryehill Coupar-Grange. On the 27th June, 1766, he married Janet, youngest daughter of Thomas Davidson, of Wolflaw, parish of Oathlaw, Forfarshire. This gentleman was born in 1705; he married Anne Curr, by whom he had one son and three daughters. Grizel, the eldest daughter, married first, James Davidson, shipmaster, Dundee; and secondly, Charles Roger, manufacturer, Dundee, (see *supra*). Margaret, the second daughter, was born in 1731, and married James Neish, merchant, Dundee; she died in 1824, leaving three sons and two daughters. The Neish family is represented by James Neish, of Laws and Omachie, and William Neish, of Clepington and Tannadice, grandsons of Mrs. Margaret Neish, or Davidson.

John, only son of Thomas Davidson, of Wolflaw, was born in 1747; he succeeded to his father's inheritance, and died unmarried in 1779, when the property was sold. Thomas Davidson was only child of Alexander Davidson, Baldragon, parish of Auchterhouse, Forfarshire, and of his wife Margaret Fleming. Alexander Davidson is alleged to have been the youngest son of Robert Davidson, of Balgay, and his wife Elizabeth Graham, a descendant of Sir William Graham of Kincardine, and a near relative of John Graham of Claverhouse, afterwards Viscount Dundee. This is stated on the authority of a member of the family now deceased, but has not been verified. The present representative of the Grahams of Claverhouse is Miss Clementina Stirling Graham, of Duntrune, the ingenious author of "Mystifications," Edin., 1865, 8vo.

Peter Roger, and his wife, Janet Davidson, had issue three sons; James and Charles, of whom hereafter, and John, born 29th March, 1772, who died in 1780; and four daughters; Anne, born July, 1769, and died in 1780; Margaret, born 17th July, 1774, died 24th November, 1858; Sophia, a twin with her brother Charles, born 5th November, 1780, died 7th May, 1822, and Isabella, born 21st April, 1777, died 23rd December, 1854. Peter Roger died 27th January, 1809, and his wife, Janet Davidson, 23rd June, 1825.

Charles, younger son of Peter Roger and Janet Davidson, was born 5th November, 1780, and died 26th March, 1865. In 1847 he published a work entitled "A Collation of the Sacred Scriptures," in which the more remarkable variations in the several English versions have been ingeniously compared. He married, first, in 1810 Isabella Allan; secondly, in September, 1817 Anne, daughter of John Cruikshank, of St. Vincent; and thirdly, in 1828, Jane Mc-Laggan; and had issue three sons, Charles, James, and Patrick, and three daughters, Anne, Sarah, and Sophia. Charles, the eldest son, published "The Rise of Canada," Quebec, 1856, 8vo. James Cruikshank, the second son, is a barrister-at-law, and F.S.A. Scot; he has contributed to the periodicals some interesting papers on Heraldry and Scottish antiquities.

James, eldest son of Peter Roger, and heir male and representative of the Roger Family in Scotland, was born on the 24th June, 1767. Having studied at the Universities of St. Andrews and Aberdeen, he obtained licence as a probationer of the Established Church on the 4th May, 1791. He was ordained minister of Dunino, in the county of Fife, on the 2nd May, 1805, and died 23rd November, 1849. He published "General View of the Agriculture of Angus, with Preliminary Observations," by George Dempster, Esq., of Dunnichen, Edin., 1794, 4to., and "Essay on Government," Edin., 1797, 8vo.; he contributed to the "Old and New Statistical Accounts of Scotland." * He married, 23rd January, 1823, Jane Haldane (born 19th January, 1804), elder daughter of the Rev. William Haldane, minister of Kingoldrum (only son of James Haldane, of Bermony), and his wife, Anna, second daughter of the Rev. Charles Roberts, presbyter of the Scottish Episcopal Church, and his wife Anne,† elder daughter of Sir John Ogilvy, Bart., of Innerquharity by his second wife, Anne,‡ daughter of James Carnegie, of Finhaven. Mrs. Jane Roger née Haldane, died 18th April, 1825, leaving an only child, Charles Rogers—the writer of these " Notes."

Having traced with some minuteness the pedigree of the eldest branch of the Scottish House of Roger, we would now adduce some particulars respecting the descent of the younger branches. A portion of the original stock of the Auldton line remained at Roxburgh till the end of the eighteenth century. In 1783, the surname appears for the last time in the register of Roxburgh parish. A branch of the family is settled in the county of Selkirk.

A branch of the Roxburghshire Family of Roger, which early settled on lands belonging to Dryburgh Abbey at Crail, Fifeshire,

* For Recollections of the Rev. James Roger, of Dunino, see "A Century of Scottish Life," Edin., 1871, 12mo., pp. 40-97.

† Mrs. Anne Roberts, née Ogilvy, married secondly John Duff, merchant, Dundee. Of this marriage were born three daughters, Innes, Barbara, and Margaret. The two latter died spinsters. Innes, the eldest daughter, became second wife of the Rev. John Skinner, Dean of Dunkeld, author of "Annals of Scottish Episcopacy," Edin., 1818, 8vo., son of Bishop John Skinner, of Aberdeen, and grandson of the Rev. John Skinner, author of "Tullochgorum." Dean Skinner was born 20th August, 1769, and died 2nd September, 1841. His widow, Mrs. Innes Skinner, née Duff, has attained her ninety-third year.

‡ A sister of Mrs. Roberts was married to Sir Robert Douglas, Bart., of Glenbervie, author of the "Peerage and Baronetage of Scotland."

and which long enjoyed a large measure of prosperity, is in the male line nearly extinct. Of a branch which settled at Edinburgh prior to the Reformation, one household seems after that event to have clung to the old faith, for in October, 1563, Christian Pynkertoun, wife of James Roger, merchant burgess in Edinburgh, was arraigned before the Justiciary Court for being present at mass in Holyrood Chapel.* John Roger, of the Canongate, Edinburgh, conformed to Protestantism ; on the 2nd December, 1564, he had his " maiden child Dorothy" baptized by the minister of the Canongate.†

A descendant of the Ochiltree Family, William Roger, settled in Ayr as a merchant, and became prosperous. Dying in January, 1578, he was succeeded by his brother Thomas Roger.‡ A son of Thomas was Parliamentary Commissioner for the burgh of Ayr ; his name as " Wilelmus Roger, pro Air," appears on the Roll of the Parliament held in Holyrood House on the 28th January, 1593. He was father of the Reverend Ralph Roger, an eminent sufferer in the cause of Presbytery. Ralph Roger was ordained minister of Ardrossan on the 27th May, 1647. Declining a call to Ayr, his native parish, he was afterwards preferred, on the invitation of the people, to the Cathedral Church, Glasgow. To this charge he was admitted on the 5th June, 1659. Having joined the Protesting party he was in October, 1662, deprived of his charge. By the Privy Council on the 7th June, 1669, he was " indulged " at Kilwinning, being the first who was so favoured. He was one of those who, on the 14th December, 1670, met at Paisley with Archbishop Leighton, with a view to an accommodation. For not observing the anniversary of the Restoration, he was fined in half his stipend, 8th July, 1673. In the year 1676 he preached in Glasgow. In the year following he presided at a meeting of " outed " Presbyterian ministers, attended both by the *indulged* and the non-indulged. On the removal of the indulgence in 1684 he was imprisoned at Edinburgh, for refusing " to give bond not to exercise his ministry in any part of Scotland." On the renewal of the indulgence in 1687 he resumed his ministrations at Glasgow. Mr. Ralph Roger died on the 3rd February, 1689. He had married, first, Margaret, daughter of Alexander

---

* Pitcairn's " Criminal Trials."

† Baptismal Register of the Canongate.

‡ Will of William Roger, merchant-burgess in Ayr, confirmed 26th September, 1598.—*Edinburgh Commissariat Register.*

Wryttowne, in Kilwinning, and, secondly, Janet Craigengelt. In his personal estate he was succeeded by his only daughter Maria.*

A member of the Ochiltree Family obtained in 1599 the lands of Wester Rossland, Renfrewshire.† His descendants acquired the adjacent lands of Hay-hill, Long-Meadows, and Gladstone, all formerly belonging to the Brisbanes of Bishoptown. The Rev. Mathew Rodger, minister of the College Church, St. Andrews, is the present proprietor of Rossland, and is lineal representative of this branch.

A branch of the Ochiltree Family settled at Glasgow,‡ and there attained considerable opulence. William Rodger was a prosperous merchant in Glasgow in 1605.§ Of that city Robert Rodger, his grandson, was Dean of Guild in 1698; he subsequently became Lord Provost, and in 1708 was elected M.P. for the burghs of Glasgow, Renfrew, Dumbarton, and Rutherglen. His son Hugh also held the office of Lord Provost.‖ Robert Rodger, son of William Rodger, wood merchant, Glasgow, and latterly a magistrate of the city, contributed to the Maitland Club a quarto volume, edited by Mr. Joseph Stevenson, entitled, "Documents illustrative of Sir William Wallace his Life and Times." His sister, Janet Rodger, married, in 1829 General Sir John Alexander Agnew Wallace, Bart., of Lochryan, a descendant of Malcolm Wallace, father of the great Scottish hero.¶

Of the Ochiltree Family a branch has long been settled in Ireland. On the 11th May, 1613,** John Roger obtained the farm of Dryan, in the barony of Raphoe, and county of Donegal, from James Cunningham, of Glengarnock, an Ayrshire landowner, who, three years before, had acquired forfeited lands in Ulster. In effecting a settlement in Ireland John Roger may have been assisted by James Lord Ochiltree, the famous chancellor, who warmly interested himself in the Scottish settlement of Ulster.†† In Ireland members of

---

* Dr. Hew Scott's "Fasti Ecclesiæ Scoticanæ." Edin., 1869, 4to., vol. ii. pp. 5, 6, 157, 181.

† In the Act of Exceptions from the Act of Indemnity passed in 1662, John Rodger, of Park, Renfrewshire, is fined £300 Scots.

‡ In Lib. Coll. Nostri Domine, Robert Roger and William Roger occur as owners of properties in Glasgow in the first half of the 16th century.

§ "View of the Merchant's House of Glasgow." Glasgow, 1856, 4to., p. 91.

‖ Anderson's "Scottish Nation," voce Roger.

¶ Burke's "Peerage," voce Wallace, Bart., of Craigie.

** Ing. Canc., Hib. Rep. ii.

†† "Correspondence of the Earl of Melrose," 4to., vol. i., p. 172.

the family occupy a respectable social status ; several are clergymen of the Irish Presbyterian Church. There is a place called Rogerstown in the county of Louth.

The armorial escutcheon of the Scottish House of Roger has not been conclusively determined. The shield of Roger du Mont Beaumont in Normandy, according to Chevillard, is argent, on a fesse sable three roses of the field, and in base three lions rampant of the second two and one, all within a bordure gules.* Quoting from Workman's MS., Nisbet assigns Roger, "of that ilk," vert on a fesse argent between three piles in chief, and a cinquefoil in base of the last—a saltier of the first. "Mr. Pont," he adds, "gives to the name of Roger only vert a fesse argent, and to another family of the name, sable, a stag's head erased argent, holding in its mouth a mullet or."† The members of the Scottish House have spelt the name variously—such as Roger, Rogers, Rodger, and Rodgers. The Coupar-Grange, or eldest branch, long maintained the original spelling, but the present representative has adopted the English form.

These Notes were incomplete without some reference to an eminent person of the name who shares with James I. the honour of originating Scottish music. Sir William Roger, or Rogers, was introduced to the court of James III. in the train of the ambassador of Edward IV. His musical abilities recommended him to the King, who appointed him president of a school of music, and in guerdon of his services granted him knighthood, and raised him to the Privy Council. To enable him to sustain his rank the king, by a charter under the Great Seal, dated 29th November, 1469, bestowed on him the lands of Traquair, forfeited by Lord Boyd.‡ The elevation of Roger and of others, whom the King on account of their accomplishments delighted to honour, exasperated the nobility, who menaced vengeance. To modify their resentment, Roger, after possessing the lands of Traquair for nine years, disposed of them at a nominal sum to the Earl of Buchan, one of the most powerful and vigorous of his opponents. On the 19th September, 1478, he executed a notarial instrument of sale in favour of Lord Buchan, dis-

---

* "Nobiliaire de Normandie," 1666, folio.

† Nisbet's "Heraldry," vol. i., pp. 59.

‡ Traquair Papers, quoted in "Chambers's History of Peeblesshire," Edin., 1864, Svo., pp. 81-86.

posing of his entire estate for seventy merks Scots, or £3 15s. 10d. sterling. But the self-denial of the musician did not avail in subduing the animosity cherished against him and the King's other favourites. In 1482, when the King was on an expedition southward to check the advance of an English army, Lord Buchan and other nobles seized on the royal favourites, and without legal form condemned them to execution. Sir William Roger was, with others, hanged at the Bridge of Lauder. "Rogers' musical compositions,"* remarks Mr. Tytler, "were fitted to refine and improve the barbarous taste of the age,* and his works were long after highly esteemed in Scotland." †

* "History of Scotland," by Patrick Fraser Tytler. Edin., 1869, 12mo., vol. ii., p. 243.

† Several seals associated with the name of Sir William Roger in Mr. Henry Laing's 'Supplementary Catalogue of Scottish Seals' (1866, 4to.), are modern forgeries.—"Notes and Queries," 1868-71, passim.

INDEX.

www.ingramcontent.com/pod-product-compliance
Lightning Source LLC
Chambersburg PA
CBHW021603270326
41931CB00009B/1356